Summer at the Beach

Learning the EA Sound

Maryann Thomas

Phonics
for the
REAL World™

Rosen Classroom Books and Materials™
New York

Do you dream of going to the beach?

You can play in the water at the beach.

You can eat a peach at the beach.

You can play in the clean sand at the beach.

9

You can swim in the sea at the beach.

You can read at the beach.

You can fish in the sea at the beach.

15

You can walk in the sand on the beach.

You can sit in a seat on the beach.

Now it is time to leave the beach.

Word List

beach

clean

dream

eat

leave

peach

read

sea

seat

Instructional Guide

Note to Instructors:

One of the essential skills that enable a young child to read is the ability to associate letter-sound symbols and blend these sounds to form words. Phonics instruction can teach children a system that will help them decode unfamliar words and, in turn, enhance their word-recognition skills. We offer a phonics-based series of books that are easy to read and understand. Each book pairs words and pictures that reinforce specific phonetic sounds in a logical sequence. Topics are based on curriculum goals appropriate for early readers in the areas of science, social studies, and health.

Vowel Digraph/Sound: ea – Make or buy flash cards of the following words: *beach, clean, dream, eat, peach, read, sea, seat.* Have the child tell how they are alike. Ask them to underline the **ea** digraph in each word. Review the alphabet, pausing at each letter to allow the child to tell if one of the above **ea** words begins with it. Have the child rearrange the flash cards in alphabetical order.

Phonics Activities: Give the child an **ea** sign card mounted on a Popsicle stick. Direct them to hold up their sign whenever you pronounce a vocabulary word with the **ea** sound. Include a few examples of different vowel sounds among the words pronounced.

- Write the **ea** vocabulary words on a chalkboard or dry-erase board. Have the child dictate a sentence using one of the words. Invite the child to trace and/or copy their sentences, illustrate them, and read them aloud.
- Make cards containing the word family *eat.* Give these to the child with individual consonant cards. Direct the child to use the cards to form new words that tell: something you do to a drum *(beat),* something the sun gives us *(heat),* something to sit on *(seat),* etc. Follow with a similar activity based upon the word *each.*

Additional Resources:

- Baxter, Nicola. *Summer.* Danbury, CT: Children's Press, 1996.
- Fowler, Allan. *How Do You Know It's Summer?* Danbury, CT: Children's Press, 1992.
- Saunders-Smith, Gail. *Summer.* Mankato, MN: Capstone Press, Inc., 1998.
- Vullo, Vera. *About Things You Find at the Beach.* Estes Park, CO: Benchmark Books, 1998.

Published in 2002 by The Rosen Publishing Group, Inc.
29 East 21st Street, New York, NY 10010

Book Design: Haley Wilson

Photo Credits: Cover, pp. 17, 21 © Peter Langone/International Stock; p. 3 © Myrleen Cate/Index Stock; p. 3 (upper right) © Volvox/Index Stock; p. 5 © Bryan Peterson/FPG International; p. 7 © David Young-Wolff/PhotoEdit/ PictureQuest; p. 9 © Telegraph Colour Library/FPG International; p. 11 © ASAP Ltd./Index Stock; p. 13 © James Lafayette/Index Stock; p. 15 © Jacob Taposchaner/FPG International; p. 19 © Bill Keefrey/Index Stock.

Library of Congress Cataloging-in-Publication Data

Thomas, Maryann.
    Summer at the beach : learning the EA sound / Maryann Thomas.
        p. cm. — (Power phonics/phonics for the real world)
    ISBN 0-8239-5950-3 (library binding)
    ISBN 0-8239-8295-5 (pbk.)
    6-pack ISBN 0-8239-9263-2
    1. Beaches—Recreational use—Juvenile literature. 2. Outdoor recreation—Juvenile literature. 3. English language—Diphthongs—Juvenile literature. [1. Beaches.] I. Title. II. Series.

GV191.62 .T56 2002
796.5'3—dc21

                                        2001000461

Manufactured in the United States of America